Designed For Speed

Written by Jenny Feely

Flying Start
to Literacy®

Contents

Introduction

Some animals can move very fast. They have strong bodies and fast-moving muscles that help them to catch their food or to avoid being eaten. They are designed for speed.

But which are the fastest animals?

Animals that move at fast speeds use a lot of energy. These animals cannot keep their speed up for very long.

Chapter 1: In water
Sailfish

The sailfish is the fastest animal in the water. It lives in the ocean. It can swim at speeds of about 110 kilometres per hour. It can reach its top speed in just a few seconds.

The sailfish folds its top fin down when it needs to swim at top speed. This makes it even faster.

The right body shape

The sailfish's body is designed to move very fast. It has a long, sleek body and a pointed bill that helps it to swim through the water easily. It has a strong tail that pushes it through the water quickly.

Colour change

Sailfish often hunt in groups. They swim rapidly into a school of fish to catch a fish to eat. If sailfish crash into each other, their sharp bills could easily cause injuries.

Sailfish can change colour to communicate with each other about what they are doing. This helps them to avoid crashing into each other.

Changing colour also confuses the small fish in a school of fish, making it easier for the sailfish to catch them.

Chapter 2: On land

Cheetahs

The cheetah is the fastest animal on land. It can run at speeds of up to 112 kilometres per hour. It can reach its top speed in less than three seconds.

Cheetahs use their speed to catch their food. They mostly eat gazelles. Gazelles are hard to catch because they can also run very fast. They can run at about 80 kilometres per hour, and they can jump high and change direction quickly.

Running fast uses a lot of energy, and cheetahs can only run at their top speed for a short time.

Long, light and strong

A cheetah's body is designed to move very fast. Its body is long and light. It has strong muscles.

When cheetahs run, they stretch out their front legs and push off hard with their back legs. They push off so hard that they often look like they are flying.

A cheetah can cover up to 7 metres in a single stride.

Running and tripping

Travelling at high speeds can be dangerous. If a cheetah crashes into its prey when it is moving fast, it can be badly hurt. The cheetah would be injured and would not be able to hunt.

To avoid crashing, the cheetah gets close to its prey. Then it reaches out its front paw and trips the animal over. The cheetah then jumps on the animal to catch it.

A cheetah tries to get close to its prey before charging. A cheetah will start to charge when it is 70 to 100 metres away from its prey.

Chapter 3: In the air
Peregrine falcons

The peregrine falcon is the fastest animal in the air. It is also faster than any other animal. Peregrine falcons hunt other birds that fly very fast, too.

When peregrine falcons dive through the air to catch their food, they can reach speeds of up to 320 kilometres per hour.

Designed for speed

A peregrine falcon's body is designed to move very fast. It can dive through the air quickly to catch its prey.

When it sees its prey, it tucks its wings, legs and tail in and dives. Its dive is called a stoop. This is the fastest way to move through the air.

The peregrine falcon's dive is called a stoop.

The peregrine falcon's beak stops the air from rushing into its body, which could damage its lungs.

The peregrine falcon also has extra eyelids. These eyelids stop dust from getting into the falcon's eyes, which would make it hard for the falcon to see.

Avoiding a crash

When a peregrine falcon dives to catch its prey, it must avoid crashing into the bird it is hunting.

To avoid crashing, the falcon stretches out its strong legs and hits one of the wings of its prey. This breaks the prey's wing so the bird cannot fly, but it does not hurt the falcon.

The injured bird falls to the ground. The falcon then flies to the ground and catches it.

Conclusion

Sailfish, cheetahs and peregrine falcons are all very fast animals. Each animal has the right body shape to help it move as quickly as possible in the places where they hunt.

Sailfish are designed to be the fastest in the water. Cheetahs have just the right body shape to be the fastest on the land. And peregrine falcons have exactly what they need to speed through the air.

They are all designed for speed.

Top 10 speeds

	Animal	Land, water or air	Top speed kilometres per hour (kph)
1	Peregrine falcon	Air	320 kph
2	Frigate bird	Air	153 kph
3	Cheetah	Land	112 kph
4	Sailfish	Water	110 kph
5	Pronghorn antelope	Land	96 kph
6	Blue wildebeest	Land	80 kph
7	Lion	Land	80 kph
8	Thomson's gazelle	Land	80 kph
9	Brown hare	Land	75 kph
10	Elk	Land	72 kph